What Do You Smell?

Seed Learning

pie

cheese

garbage

diaper

soap

popcorn

garlic

socks

What do you smell?

I smell popcorn.

What do you smell?

I smell cheese.

What do you smell?

I smell dirty socks.

Let's learn about Mexico.

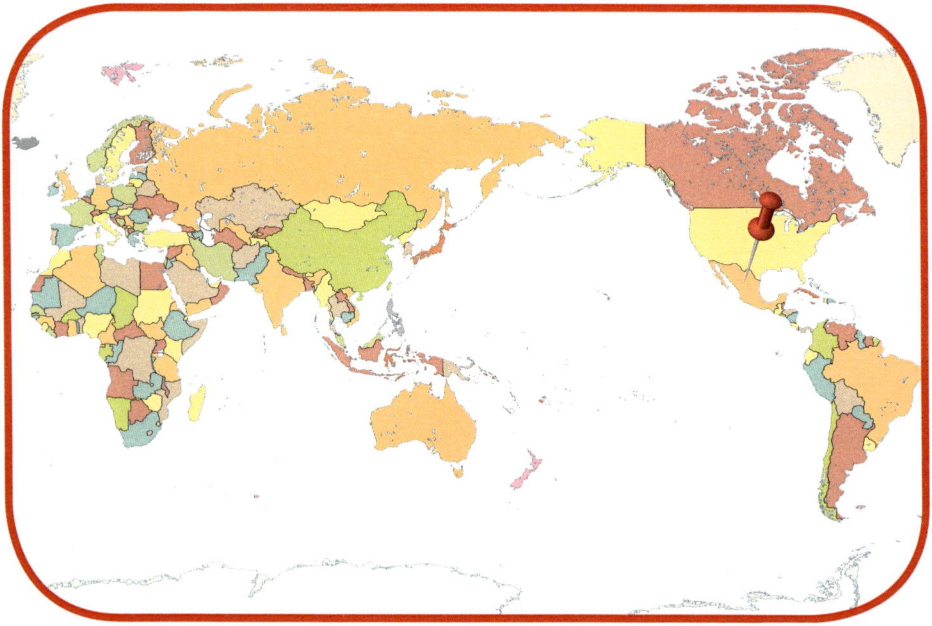

Flag of Mexico

Sombrero